i am

BLACK

EMAN NEPAY

i am

BLACK

EMAN NEPAY

ISEEBOOKZ PUBLISHING LLC
LAGRANGE, GEORGIA

I AM BLACK

iSeebookz Publishing LLC
Suite 300 Commerce Ave Ste 137B
LaGrange, GA. 30241

Publication creation was completed by iSeebookz Publishing Services.
Interior Design: Priscilla Sodeke
Book cover: Tananykina Svetlana/Shutterstock

ISBN: 978-1-7347762-4-9

Printed in the United States of America

First edition
10 9 8 7 6 5 4 3 2 1

POETRY CONTENT

DEDICATED TO MY ANCESTORS

Because of your sacrifice, I am. My sincere wish is to be in favor of your blessings as you sit high, looking low. May your wisdom rest upon us, enlightening our minds during our trying times.

A special dedication to Yvette, your resilience to live became my inspiration in your return to the spirit world. May our ancestors love you with open arms as you rest.

Eman Nepay

We Matter

Our justice is due. Our justice is not at the expense of you.
Our lives matter despite the status quo
Our lives matter regardless of what you think and know.
Our story is yet to be told
Our story is costly as it unfolds
We will not be your stomping ground any more
We will be our own

Black life matter
Black life thrives
Despite the guns shot against our back!
Black life matter
Black life survives
Despite the lack

Who are we that you fear us so?
Police brutality is our daily reality.
Who are we that our disparity is ratings?
Portrayed before society
We will not be denied
Our time has come
To stand as destiny has designed.
Our time has come
Your day of ruling us is done

We will not go
Where Jim Crow has sown
We will not trail toward an era
I am not a MAN.
I am not human
I am less than
I am not worthy
Of living with dignity!

Those days have come and gone
Kill us in the streets
Demonize us as we speak
But we will not be denied.

Our history has shown we are not so docile
To let you walk over us without feeling our guile.
We shall survive. We will thrive
black LIFE, our LIFE, MATTERS!

Written by Y.D. ROWLAND THE WRITER 2020

A SPECIAL THANKS

To my publishing manager, "she who should not be named!"
To the service providers at iSeebookz Publishing LLC, because of
your support, my dreams are becoming a reality.
Best wishes to you all. This page is just for you.

Sincerely,

Eman Nepay

*Fear, the emotional standard of neglecting the exceptional courage
needed to overcome the adversity of the inner soul,
while reflecting on the thoughts of the mind.*

Eman Nepay

The Foundation

*"In the beginning God created the heaven and the earth. And the
earth was without form, and void; and darkness was upon the face
of the deep. And the Spirit of God moved upon the face of the waters.
And God said, Let there be light: and there was light. And God
saw the light, that it was good: and God divided the light from the
darkness. And God called the light Day, and the darkness he called
Night. And the evening and the morning were the first day."*

GENESIS 1:1–5

*"In the beginning was the Word, and the Word was with God, and
the Word was God. The same was in the beginning with God. All
things were made by him; and without him was not any thing made
that was made. In him was life; and the life was the light of men."*

JOHN 1:1-4

I am the master of myself! My flesh is subjected to the laws of the
Universe. The Universal Intelligence that resides within is called life, and it
comes from the spiritual realm. I do not allow others to define me. I am my
own person. Personal opinions are not relevant when lacking wisdom or
truth that illuminates minds to change.

I do not allow others to tell me who I am. I am who I am. I do not live for acceptance. I live to breathe, and on my last breath, I hope to reflect upon the wonders of living. I am anticipating the promise of an afterlife experience, connecting to the eternal source of my being. I reject status quo thoughts, a system of man who took my name, my language, my culture, my religion, my GOD, and used my lack for the exploitation of my demise.

I paint my portrait with the paint provided by a spiritual walk. Thus I denounce the status quo and their gods, the god of money, superiority, greed, slavery, dishonesty, genocide, and dependence.

I have my OWN GOD, and this GOD speaks to me.

I bow down to the God of understanding, equality, love, harmony, prosperity, and independence. I bow down to the God who sees me as a whole, who made me an individual with choices and rights. I bow to the God that gave me value, and to be of value for a purpose to fulfill. I am a being designed by THE CREATOR, THE GOD of universal laws, that cannot be changed or manipulated through time. THIS GOD has no respect of persons. THIS DIVINE created a world after bathing in darkness, birthed the light, and gave all its creation essence of life.

Life the universal intelligence can't be fully understood in the mind of man. Is it a spirit, a FORCE uniquely designed to run a timed course? What will it transcend beyond this realm? The questions remain a mystery, and one thing holds true: man has no control.

Thus I am the master of myself. The Essence of Eternity resides in me. I kneel to the God that gave its essence for me to be a living being. This God is not the portrait of a man centuries ago painted as blond and blued eyed. IT is more than two thousand years old and transcends beyond the word deity dating back six thousand years.

This God created time and allows for the endless thoughts of man. This God, no man understands! Man can only perceive through finite thinking, WHILE GOD THOUGHTS ARE eternal. How ludicrous of us to say we know and comprehend the mind of THE CREATOR. We are simple-minded beings in comparison to who GOD IS!

I bow humbly to say ALL HONOR TO THE CREATOR. I PRAY for the grace to become enlightened with wisdom, understanding, specifically designed, to transcend limited thought programmed by man.

MY God is beyond the rhetoric of man and his attempt to explain the mysteries of the SUPREME BEING. Man's ignorance to control and shape the minds of people, to do a distorted will, has capitalized God for greed overflowing. Man has desecrated GOD's image, painting God as a fake, a slave master, a lover of money, a facilitator of favoritism, and unreachable except through the system of the status quo process.

GOD'S existence is an enigma. Its beginning may have been before time and will be after time is no longer in existence. IT IS the true Alpha and Omega. THIS GOD follows an order that man has broken down, an order that must be rebuilt with eternal truth. A truth that mandates the beginning was basic life-sustaining itself without man's help. All things received and gained and needed; God gave in the beginning.

SO to the seekers of truth and love, the time has come! The flood gate of truth is spilling on the ground with every unjust death. Love is crying in the wind with every protest against every unjust law, an action of our times! The waters are melting, bringing fresh water from glaciers high, and from the depths of our earth, to wash away the toxins of our living. Embrace the new day embrace being BLACK. For we are all one hue, we are the seekers of truth." SO let's go back to our origins, the origins of our essence from an Eternal source. BEING ONE WITH THE MASTER OF LIFE... we were here when God commanded: "Let there be light."

I AM BLACK...

A SPIRITUAL WALK

Religion

The ongoing slavery of the mind
Are countless images portraying Love's divine.
The shrines that we leave
Worship buildings
Left dormant ninety-six hours
Weeks at a time.

Religion,

The prayers we pray
Hoping for a change in some way.
Yet the money is honey
For those in control the
Pastors and deacon boards.

Religion,

Keeps us in the box
Always looking out,
Sunday morning exercise
And all the women shout.

Religion,

A higher level of thinking
Would be sublime.
But religion,
The slavery of our times
Doesn't seek to bring
The true enlightenment of the mind

Is This The Word?

We put him in a box, all nice and pretty
Then the ministers say, live a life that is fitting.
We say we adore him and lavish him with blessings.
We sit and hope to gain life's riches

The ministers say we must worship him each day.
We faithfully, daily, sit, and humbly pray

This all sounds good, from day-to-day
Makes us feel proud and righteous, to continue this way

God is love. God is peace,
HE is joy, knows our every toil.
God is patient. God is kind,
HE knows what he did when he created mankind.

God is jealous. God is strong,
Won't sit back, and do nothing when He sees wrong

God is active. He's everywhere. He is in the air we breathe,
He fights for a righteous humanity.

God is a creator He created all of this.
He strategically fights, to keep what is his!

God said let us make man, in our image-
a piece of himself, he blew within us.

Man he made, the woman he created.
Have dominion and reign, to them, is what he stated.

A simple command, obedience demanded
Worship him, in spirit, and in truth
What became of the statement, he commanded us to do?
A child of God, we're titled today!
Do you think God sees us in this way?

Look at the children of God today
Have we been obedient and continued in God's way?

We don't make trouble. We keep the peace,
But we won't stand up, against our countries inhumanity!

We are civil and will turn the other cheek
Do we understand, what HE meant, when HE said blessed are the meek?

We do unto others, as we'd want them to do unto us.
And keep our mouths shut when we see injustice.

We bridle our tongue and watch the world's wrongs
We pray to God to take care of it all.
When do we think we should get involved?

We say we are a child of God.

Why did He create, two hands, two feet and
Two eyes that we may see?

What a disgrace to NOT act IN HIS way,
Yet we say we love God each day!

Love him and pray day and night,
And fail to fight for what is right.

Listening to ministers, of today,
What's so important that they have to say?
That we forget the one commandment,
God gave on our blessed birthday!

He blew into us a piece of himself,
Sad to say, we don't exercise that gift
In every way

A PERSONAL REFLECTION

Poetry in motion

Can you say you KNOW me?
This inner being
A spark away from life and death
Because of me, YOU exist.

This inner being
Left to its demise
Heal's beats and breaths for you

Do you really know me?

I who formed in your mother's womb
A tiny piece from the heavens above
Cursed or blessed to this existence
The maker of my hell or heaven
On this planet called Earth
In this place, we call mother

Do you know me?

I am the inner you
I commune with you daily
Yet have you discovered

The infinite wisdom
I have within ready to give?

Creation

In darkness,
We sat among brethren
Awaiting our time...

Bathing in the liquid of life,
We communed with sisters,
Engulfed in the blackness of night.

Embracing maturity...

As brethren, we journeyed far across wetlands.
Up rapid streams to find solace.
As sisters, we mourned the departure of our elder
As she journeyed to resting shores

Journeyed travelers...

Brethren in groups,
Remembered their training
Elder sister sat
As a lady waiting

The meeting was their inevitable fate.

Time was of the essence
12 hours to be exact.
Elder sister sat in tranquility
As brethren fought defensively.

Brethren died and lost their way,
Only one maybe two would find their ultimate mate.
And dance the ancient song ...

World's populace at stake...

Elder sister summoned travelers,
As they approached her resting shores
Her embrace would be obtained.

An ageless ritual of conception,
The continuation of our existence.
The traveler's essence, merging to one.

This being is called life... The continuation of MAN...
Egg and sperm the first mating of our existence.

The Unknown

The blood-stained sheets met me
It greeted me in the midst of the pain
It pushed at the edges of my brain

The forces trying to break free,
The plays of life hurdles keeping me

At the door of poverty!

The cries of the poor
The children that sleep
Bellies filled with air
Cause cupboards are bare

The pain of the man, who has no place to rest,
Due to the nag who lay on his chest...

The woman who settles for less
Making bread CRUMBS her worth
Forget she is one with the Creator to give birth.

WAKE UP!

In us resides the innate ability
Step out of the box
Demand your right to be
We are born with all the things we need
To make it in this world living free.

HEAL!

Create and invent,
Forget the naysayers,
The thoughts of negativity
The negative thoughts of not,
Stand in the energy of I can do...

STOP!

STAND!

For your life moves by the actions of your feet
The current of electricity flowing through your being,
Transformed itself to the manifestations of your success
Or what you deem your failures.

BE!

For you are not what the world thinks you are
You are more than what you deem yourself to be.
You are a manifestation of a universe wrapped.
In the cosmos of this thing called human (BEING)

You are the energy that set the motion of the ocean.
The energy that flows in the breeze,
The energy that sat with God himself
And watched the first fish draw its water breath.

THE ONE TO MAKE LIFE WHAT YOU WANT IT TO BE!

Not what your mother or father the alcoholic said you'd never be
You are One who will nurture the motherless child
Even though a monster took your virginity,
Leaving the scar of barren land in the womb called life.
You are the one to take the stand and fight.

You are the chosen...

That blood-stained sheets greeted in the midst of pain.
Guided and pushed as the edges of your brain.
Forced to break free, from the world of spirit
To the land of human being,

You are the one BIRTHED!

What Holds You?

What

holds

you

back?

lack of knowledge
money
fear of the next step

SAY NO MORE!

learn
earn
take the step

It

is

as

simple

as

that!

You Don't Know my Pain

You don't know my pain.
I smile, just like yesterday never came.

You don't know how I feel
The wretched heartache
Not seeing what true love is again.

I will talk to you
But you don't know my inner thoughts
The silent tears that bleed
From my grieving heart

My actions do not speak anguish,
The deep and open wound
That no one can console
Etched within my soul.

My everyday dues of living,
I practice without everyone knowing.
I am a spirit in mourning.

My private thoughts...

The countless unspoken issues of my life
That I have taken in stride, in the midst of strife
The countless sleepless nights
The watered pillows that dry by days' light

So while some will sit and look with disdain
Unable to see with natural eyes
The inner working of the soul of this man

Maybe in time, you will understand
When judgment day makes it plain
You Don't Know My Pain!

Been There Done That

Ever been in so much pain, emotionally and physically
You just wanted to check out on life?

Been there felt that...

Ever been talked about so bad
By people who didn't have a clue
Of who you really are
And all you could do was pray?

Been there done that...

Have you ever had a dream
That you kept to yourself and
Silently you made it a reality?
Cause by talking about it
The naysayers would have killed it.

Been there done that...

Have you ever looked around at your life
Happy with its results, but others won't let you live?

Been there done that...

Have you ever just looked at people
Saw their motives and questioned why me,
Just to think... how others could have it worse than you?

Been there felt that...

Have you ever read a poem thinking this is me...
And you realize it was about the writer...
Been there and we don't walk alone,
We have ...done that!

Untold

I am an adult who holds to themselves
The greatest of secrets I take to my grave.

No one would ever know due to my fear
I am a mother, a father, alienated from family and friends.
Ostracized to keep the dark secret that I abhorred
The darkest secret since my childhood

It's the worst secret to keep, as it eats away at the core of my being.
What I endured, only those who have been in my place, will understand.

There is no solace except for that which I give
Grateful for my faith to survive willed by strength to live

The pain I have endured has led to years of insecurity,
Trust issues and the pain of questioning love's reality?

My sorrow is the silent tears at night,
The vivid dreams that haunt me in daylight

They are nightmares of events revisited in my sleep
I am the adult living a silent trauma that I have to keep.

I am a health care provider, a social worker,
A librarian, an ex-convict,
A construction worker and a teacher

I am the child in the wee hours of the night,
Or in the light of day,
That had its innocence taken away!

I am that one that rose above it all
I stand able to put in perspective,
I am not my past, though it haunts me with dread.

You will never know I was XXXXXXXX.

Ourselves

We struggle within ourselves
To free ourselves from ourselves
Never realizing it is because of ourselves
We are...

We become beings to prove ourselves
To the world to make ourselves something
Yet we never come to grips with ourselves
And thus we lose ourselves
In trying to be something...

We want for our selves
And strive to achieve to get for selves
Yet we fail ourselves.
Never understanding that within ourselves
Is the key to ourselves
Thus we are lost trying to achieve
That which is within!

Peace of Mind

Looking up at the gray clouded day,
We think of all our naysays.

We reminisce about the many of you,
The can't conversations, and you'll never do.

The nothing special's
we'll amount to.

Yet here we sit,
Looking down upon those stones

The negativity
That paved the way
To my productivity...

The ultimate foundation,
Of my success today...

A LIFE GIVEN

Appreciation

Life is so beautiful,

I wonder how many of us really appreciate

This gift given to us called LIFE.

Do we appreciate the breath we breathe?

The movement of muscle that allows us to move

The spirit that courses through this vessel called the body.

It is a world of its own systems organized to function.

We are all connected.

Life is greater than our individuality.

It is our unity that strengthens us.

One

The Earth washes
Water,
over
The Spirit of One.

The nature of Earth
Gives life!

The Mother of us all,
Calls for us to wonder,
It beckons us to dream!

Become one with all that is around us,
As OUR ancestors for centuries esteemed...

Sacred Being

The scent of her embrace on our darkest of days!
A sacred being, who gave us life
No one can surpass her sacrifice.

From her womb to this world, we breathe.
From the skinned knee
To the matters of the heart
She has been with us, from the start.

Your first heartbeat
The first breath you took
No one can compare
Her being is so rare.

For all, you have taken in stride
All you have accomplished
While beaming with pride
You can't deny,
This woman's sacrifice.

Whether in the present or distant past...
Mother the name, will always last!
A thank you won't be enough
For all, she has done for us.

For my Mother

No one can understand
How much love I hold within
Years have passed and all the love and advice
Have paved the way for my life...

Regrets I may have
Missing your laugh or a smile as the years went bye.
A little wrinkle here or there
Gray that appeared with each passing year...

People may say how a mother could act this way
Leaving her children to go her own way
Leaving children to grow and not be in there life every day

To you, I say, yes, the years have passed...

Regrets we may have
Missing your laugh or a smile as years have gone by
A wrinkle or two may have appeared on your face

But we as children can not forget.
The years of you wiping our tears, calming our fears.
The endless smiles, the stern look as you swiped our behinds
After doing things that were to our demise
You made us who we are...wise

You gave us life
You instill in us a sense of pride
We knew we had your love
Your presence has always been with us in our hour of need
The wisdom you gave in our growing years we have redeemed

You are the sacred mother
From whence we came
You shall be cherished always.

WITH LOVE

Compassion And The Hypocrite

Compassion is a divine gift to man.
It's appalling he doesn't understand

This gift only a Supreme Being
Could present to a charlatan.

Yes, it is to you I speak,
Those who think they are wise counsels,

Who are not concerned about humanity.
Habitually look down upon the creation of the Almighty,
As if you are in authority.

But then I understand that the Charlatan
Can't have compassion for his fellow man

Unless he has made a treaty,
To follow in the footsteps of the Almighty.

So I don't fault you, Hypocrite for trying to replicate,
The most divine gift to man

Seeing that you don't understand,
how to put into action Compassion.

Marriage A Decade In Time

A decade is about time
The time of seeing the same ole face
But happy to see it just the same....

The time of questions...
"Did you lower the seat?"
"Are you listening to me?"
"Girl, don't you see the game on TV?"

A decade is about acceptance...
"You know I wanted that done last week."
"Did you clean the gutters and sweep the street?"
"Man, help me fold these clothes."
"Woman, don't close the door, I have a lot more."

A decade is about understanding...
"I heard you cry last night."
"Come, I need you by my side."
"Baby, it's going to be alright!"

It is about love...
Not the wining and dining.
Nor whose right over more wrong...
It is a wait in the waiting room...
And joys of seeing a child being born...

A decade is about dedication,
Of time passed, looking back,
Remembering the slack,
Joy from making that bonus check!
Going from PB and J's to eating at the restaurant called Ray's!

A decade is about time...
Time of acceptance and understanding
That love is all about our personal dedication.

So What can I say about two people married for a decade...
Happy to say ten years was made, and in 15 more years.
I pray for more happy memories...
So we can come back,
To celebrate a quarter of a century...

Auditioning

I am not auditioning for that low rise,
You wish to place into my prize,
Oh, silly male, you are...

I only climb to the highest peak of my reach,
Climaxing only by the parting of your lips,
The truth you speak...

Foreplay the greeting sound,
Of your morning speech... a simple hello,
For you realize I am more precious than Gold.
Your value is weighed by how much of your life is told.

My heart is racing while watching,
Your mind embracing knowledge and scholar debating,
Hm... I am masturbating.

In a library with your understanding of the universe,
Celestial stars and planets.
I'm relating,
To sunsets and warm beach strolls
Feeling the sand between my toes.

I am climbing to the highest peak of my reach,
Climaxing, on the truth you speak,
Embracing the same knowledge that you seek!

Now let's do some parting within the sheets.
Only Your mind... Is what I will need.
For I am not auditioning for that low rise,
You wish to place into my prize,
Oh, silly male, you are...

Ignorant

Intelligence wilted by the lack of knowledge that if

Given time to search within for a

Noteworthy habit to derail the aspects of

Oppressing the light of wisdom to

Revive your brain's gray matter to

Accept a reality that your

Negative concept of thinking reinforces a warped

Truth that inhibits the enlightenment of the mind...

THE STORY

AFRICAN ORIGINAL

who am I

An unknown name with a
Fake language and a
Reformed history
Institutionalized
Conforming
Abnormally to a society that still calls me
Nigger, some are

Obviously offended
Remembering
Intellectually illicitly my
Genealogy... they are
Ill-tempered, knowing by
Nature
All DNA, our
Longevity started with me ...

So Who am I

I am my DNA
I am Your story
I claim the first soul.

I am an **AFRICAN ORIGINAL**

Temper Tantrum

I am the child denied,
Denied to say who I really am inside.
I am a toddler not wanting to share,
The very ideas and concepts of all that is fair

My name defamed, and my time can't be reclaimed.
My ancestors of Africa's past from Egypt to Johannesburg,
No, I don't want to hear my DNA is shared with everybody.
I want to claim it as my own.
Since the time of claiming has been taken from
The lost African on American shores.
The least my brothers and sisters could do,
Is bequeath me the time to accept my due,
Without having to share with the lighter hue,
Who denied me my TRUTH....

I know we are all one.
But at this time, I am the child denied,
Denied to say who I really am inside.
I am the toddler not wanting to share,
Forgoing all that you deem should be fair.

I don't want to share my ancestry of Africa's past,
From Egypt to the tip of what was once KEMET

No Ramses or Nefertiti Pharaohs of Egyptian Dynasty.
It isn't a fantasy, they looked like this black me.
The rest of the world just doesn't want it to be...
Everybody already has a piece of me...

For if you look back on African soil,
There you will see the real me.
A lineage of luxury the real royalty
That gave to the world technology.
And the life we deem to humanity.

We are all one

We are all one
This can't be undone!

For within us is the essence of all humanity.

Colors of man, Black, Brown, Red, White
We are all Mother Natures creations in sight.

Different hues we adorned
Different cultures we have learned
Different languages we have embraced
Though we are all still of the human race...

NO superiority or inferior views
No matter to your color hue
All life deserves its due...

Value to all it can't be denied
Value to all that dipped its essences in the Nile
We are all one this can't be undone...

Red, Brown, Black, and White
We are all brothers and sisters in creations sight
Mother Nature's uniqueness, all to her delight...

We have a lifetime to make it right
Unconditional love to all within our sight

DIPPED *"We are all one 2.0"*

We all dipped in the waters of the Nile.

It can't be denied
We are all one

This can't be undone.

For within us is the essences that make us
Brother, sister, the family of Human life...

Different hues we adorn

Our travels to distance shores

Changed the surfaces of our hands!

White, Red, Brown, Black man...

We are all brothers and sisters in creations sight...

Mother Nature's uniqueness, all to her delight

Her children all dipped in the waters of the Nile!

It can't be denied.

Transcends Color Lines

There is something magical
About the human spirit
That transcends color lines.

Racial cultures that touch
Hearts and minds.

People that seek to understand
The harmony that we all are one.

An energy source broken into pieces
Spread across the globe.

As we exhale we give back to ourselves
The essence of the energy...

As we reach out and touch lives
Relating and Connecting
Particles of an eternal source.

We travel across space and
Our light shines bright!

We Transcend moments called time
And we are color blind...

What Do You See?

Look into the mirror, and what do you see?
Big lips broad nose and short kinky hair
Wide hips, thick thighs, and maybe a butt on the backside...
Brown skin, black skin, dark skin all near cocoa brown
Don't you dare frown or hold your head down!

Look into my mirror,
And you will see
That our story is richer beyond your dreams.
Look into the mirror,
Don't you dare drop your eyes or hold your head down and frown
For your ancestors wore crowns
The Kings and Queens, scholars, scientist
Explorers of the world-renowned.

Our story doesn't all begin on the shores of American soil.
Some would have you to believe.
That slavery is our beginning,
Less than, beneath, not worth living in the lap of luxury
That we were better off not being free.

But let me tell you our story, for our beginning, is yet to be told.
Look to the east and you will see
The pyramids, the Sphinx
Tall statues of men and women looking like you and me
That lived in the lap of luxury
So rich, that the statues were made over hundreds of centuries
And they still stand for the entire world to see.

Don't you dare hold your head down!
Big lips, broad nose, and short kinky hair
Wide hips, thick thighs and a big butt on the backside...
Brown skin, black skin, dark skin.

For over in the east on the shores
Be our land our kinsmen's origin
Of our motherland...Rich in gold, diamonds,
Oil, our fertile soil.
Some would have you to believe
That a spear and a loincloth is all, we adorned.
Think East, our African land, where we were once free

Living in the laps of luxury
NASA ain't got nothing on me
For its symbol came from a mind
That DNA resides within me.
The confederate flag in all due respect...
The pharaohs crossed their arms, in rest making that X.

Love Sambho, not sambo the blackened white face bimbo
But the God deity that summons all to a higher level of humanity.

Keep the Nigger word, I'll embrace Naga,
For it is defined as the powerful life force
Passed down through generations
The wisdom of the Great Divine source.

...

Visit the museum, and you will see
Caskets made of gold where our kings laid to rest
Tombs one of the many pyramids to the east
Not a 6 by 6 feet hole in the cemeteries we see.

If you look around you'd be amazed
At all the things your ancestors gave...

So don't you hold your head down, don't you dare frown
Big lips, broad nose, and short kinky hair
Wide hips, thick thighs, and maybe a butt on the backside...
Brown skin, black skin, dark skin all near cocoa brown.

For you are the legacy, the future of your ancestry
While you may have been stripped
From Your native land carried over on ships.
Packed like sardines in a can
Prisoners to work for another man.

Hold your head up, look straight toward the horizon
Though shackled and chained in prison is where your father lays
You are the future of your ancestry

That lived in the lap of luxury so rich
That the statues were made over hundreds of centuries
And they still stand for the entire world to see.

Where Aristotle and Socrates
The great thinkers and philosophy of Greece
Came to our shore to learn from thee.
The THEE that resides within you and me
The DNA passed down through centuries.

For we are royalty
Here's some advice from the heart...
Reading writing and arithmetic
That ain't just a white man's art
Our people were teaching this
Before Greece was even a thought!

So hold your head up, look straight toward the horizon
For you are the legacy, the future of your ancestry
Look to the east and see,
What was made by us over hundreds of centuries...
Statues that look like you and me...
And they still stand for the entire world to see...

Big lips, broad nose, and short kinky hair
Wide hips, thick thighs, and maybe a butt on the backside...
Brown skin, black skin, dark skin all near cocoa brown
For your ancestors wore crowns
The Kings and Queens, scholars and scientist
Explorers of the world-renowned!

W
  H
    A
      T

   D
    O

      Y
        O
          U

            SEE?

Privilege

As you flaunt your white privilege
Being the star of billboards
Media and history books.

My child silent wishes to be you
Quietly is being programmed to see you
The epitome of life standards
Due to the lack of seeing themselves constantly!

So, I don't apologize for showing my pride
Fist raised parading, I'm black, and I'm proud,
As I walk the street

I have to countersue
The ongoing picture of seeing your hue
And all the things you deem
To the detriment of me
In regards to you

You Offend

You offend me with your lies, your eyes are full of deceit.
There is no love for the hatred you have shown me.
You wish for the blinded eye, the dumb stare.
Then Jesus blessed art the meek glare.
I can't stand the thought of perpetuating your disease.
You are granted an appease.

Don't shout stand on your own two feet.
Get a job stop blaming whitey. Welfare food stamps loving black foe.
You took from me my right to vote, to elevate, and to progress my community.

Have you forgotten our story from 1895 to 1923?
How about our story whitewashed for centuries?
Don't want to publish that in American books for world history.
It's too black and too strong...
It will shed light on your 13-19th century's wrongs!

So sick of seeing you.
Cause you have no thoughts of being fair
By giving righteous men their due
It's sad to say you fed over your poor kinsmen too.
Made them feel superior to the very people that make you feel inferior.

We have no animosity toward white brothers, who understand,
We all are created man in this great nation.
They have, in unity, stood for the right of all God's creations.

But to the lot of you,
Still dripping with the ignorance of years past,
I wish I had the right to whip you natural prejudice racist ass.

In My Mind

I sit thinking thoughts of You.
They are so profoundly negative it should astound You,
But then again, maybe not.

See I smile, I'm cordial,
I'm reticent and yes,
I keep my emotions in check.

However just below the surface,
Deeply rooted in my entire being,
It is an aversion to You.
A wave of righteous anger that wants to break through.

Yes, I have thoughts of You...

When I sit in classes
When I stand on any given corner,
And turn around just to see You.

My inner man cries; it burns to get back at You.
You, who imitate and continue to exercise,
The atrocities granted to my people!

Yes, I think thoughts of You.

Too Black Too Strong

I can't be Sambo, it goes against my nature.
I'm too black and too strong, and I have a mind of my own.

I can't be your child's mammy that too goes against my belief and
Inevitably leaves a sour feeling in my entire being.

No, I can't be your house nigger
See first I need my own space and
When I look in the mirror
I don't see your nigger written on my face.

No, your history won't do!
Too much of you and too little of me,
See, I look back, and I see my story plainly.
You just don't want the rest of the world to see clearly.

No, I can't stand your ways.
Like God, my thoughts are not your thoughts.
And my ways are not your ways.
And unlike you, I'm not afraid of how my mind was made.

Yes, I am too black and too strong, like God.
I can't go along with all your wrongs.

Yes, I am too black and too strong, like God.
I can't allow you to cause my people more harm.

Yes, I am too black and too strong and like God
You have to come correct or leave me the Hell alone!

Derogatory Ally or Foe

Cracker Please
Nigger Please
An ally or a foe?
The time has come; we can't tell it anymo'.

Stroller pushed by pink skin, a caramel baby held within...

Cracker, please
Nigger, please
An ally or a foe?
Our time has come; we can't tell anymo'.

Grandma at a checkout stand
Grandpa at carnival land
Hand in hand caramel child smiles
And they understand...

What was once a taboo...
Has come to haunt a few...
Yet to grandma and grandpa,
It's a child's wonder and awe!

Cracker Please
Nigger Please
An ally or a foe?
The times have changed, and we can't tell no mo.'

A Black man dies...
White man screams...
The anguish of their mother is heard in the streets...

Cracker, please
Nigger, please
An ally or a foe?

What was once the status quo,
Ain't here no more...

An impregnated Black woman
From a black man,
Their white child born,
Don't you understand...

Cracker Please
Nigger Please
We are an Ally, not a foe!

Can we not use these
Derogatory terms anymo'!

OUR STORY

BLACK

What do I write to a world
Not ready for my strife!

This word I speak
To the life of this thing called being...

Neither the mild nor the meek...
Will come to seek
From the wisdom that I speak...

For this gift I give
Can only come from being free
Not from the form of the bondage
That makes a man flee!

No, you can not see me.
For I am the countless speck of a being
Connected to the spirit of infinity...

I AM BLACK

My Story

Black History dipped in racism,
Screaming terrorist as a day is long,
Centuries of injustice,
That no judge can make undone

My story will sicken you to the core,
And have you praying for peace to your creator.

This history tainted with sins has last,
Stands tall and transcends the soils of America's past.

My Black history while it is all the above,
It is one that has shown, people, love.

THIS history will enlighten your mind...

From my native land to western shores,
Shackled, chained, Denied my name...
Yet my history can not be contained.

I am the I am.
I was in the beginning,
I will be in the end.

Conceited?
Blasphemy?
NAY I Proclaim...

To You, I say...
Study man...
The being of Human...

Give Me Black

Give me black
The darkest color of crayon.

The blackest of night
Where my eyes can't see the light

Give me black
The darkest of dirt
Where the soil is rich
The mother earth
Where the first man from God was birthed!

Give me black
Royal dynasty
Places God resides
The first place before, let there be light!

Give me black
Hooded men on Spanish soil
Holy monks, adornment stole?

Give me black
Religion of Christianity
Egyptian philosophy?

Give me black
Cush and Kemet
Ethiopia and the world,

Give me black...

Rwanda

The pain of the slain
The cries of the children
The genocide of love and
The birth of hatred, breed
From a fountain of superiority

We look the same,
Our nose is broad
Our skin is dark and yet,
We killed in....

Rwanda,

The blacks in the world
No matter where we are
Exist.....

Rwanda,

Prejudice lynching in America
Apartheid in South Africa
Injustice in Australia
Unrest in France
No peace in the Middle East
Racism worldwide all demonstrate...

Rwanda,

The pain of the slain
The cries of the children
The genocide of love and
The birth of hatred, breed
From a fountain of superiority...

How many of the darker hue must
Die before we feel the effects
Of a genocide left to its own demise
Like...

Rwanda,

The blacks in the world
No matter where we are
Exist.....

Rwanda,

And the world again closes its eyes and
Rwanda's spirit lifts its head and rise.
Sudan comes into view. The white hue,
You who programmed and fashioned
A state of being, silently sit and watch
The genocide you demised....

The pain of the slain
The cries of the children
The genocide of love and
The birth of hatred, breed
from a fountain of superiority...

Remember the Middle Passage,
Remember the Slave Trade,
Remember these holocausts
Remember Rwanda...

A Time To Mourn

I'm mourning
And tears are rolling down my face.
I saw him hanging from a tree.
My ancestor back in 1803

I'm mourning
And tears are rolling down my face.
I saw my ancestor's charred body
At the county square, a white girl stared
With a smiling glare

I'm mourning
And tears are rolling down my face.
I thought about my ancestor,
Who was hung from a tree,
Her child's life was cut from her belly.

I'm mourning
And tears are rolling down my face.
I saw my female ancestor used,
Rape is what they call that abuse.

I'm mourning
And tears are rolling downing my face.
The story of an ancestor running away
Trying to get to freedom in any way.

I am mourning
And the tears continue to run down my face...
Free in body, tortured in mind...
You'll never understand what it takes to be black in this nation.

I'm mourning, and tears are rolling down my face...

Break Free

I am the voice of those wanting to break free.

Break free of the negativity.

Breaking free of prejudice due to,

color,
race,
religion,

inequality toward humanity.

Breaking free of the strains of life.

Breaking free of all the strife!

I am more than what others think of me.

I am breaking free.

Living the life that is within.
Manifesting the best of my potential, regardless of men.

For I reflect the HE
The Universal ESSENCE
Who made me.

Move On

Move on, you say, Move from what?

Can you give me back my language, my culture,
My connection with my family from the past?
Can you give back the life that was lynched,
The years of discrimination and ongoing prejudice?

Move on, move on from what?

Can you remove the genocide,
That has been done worldwide?
Can you bring back...
The Black Wall Street mentality of our community?
Can you bring back...
Communities that had the chance to be apart of our longevity

Move on. Move on from what?
Burned down houses, the lynched men, and
Fetuses cut from the belly of pregnant black women.

Move on, you say! Move on from what?

A week, now a month, how about all year long,
Black history where our credit is truly due
The contributions to this nation
Placed on the white of hue.

Move on from what?

Move on from the inferiority complex drilled in the mind.
Our past that we must overcome in spite of you.

Move on... Move on from what?

The lives lost at sea, the middle passage,
Plantation existence, No reparation
You dare to have the audacity to tell me...

MOVE ON. MOVE ON!!!
BRING BACK! GIVE BACK!
ALL THAT YOU TOOK!
only then, will i move on.

Forgive and Forget

How can you ask me to forget?
How dare you assume,
I will forgive for your conscious to reign clear.
I do neither.
I forgive for my own peace of mind.

I will never forget.

To forget is to disrespect the death of my ancestors of the past.
To forget is to dishonor those who came before me,
Who paved the way for my liberties.
To forget is to dismiss the injustices done to my people.
How dare you ask me to forget?
How dare you assume,
I will forgive for your conscious to reign clear

I love those who love me as I am.
I love those who see me as an equal.
I love those who understand,
The true meaning of brotherhood!
To those, I forgive, their ancestors.
For their iniquity who see me with equality

I hate those who hate me.
I don't give you the benefit of the doubt.
You are not innocent until proven guilty.
You are guilty in my eyes until you prove otherwise.
Your character is judged until you show yourself worthy of my trust.
Blame my thoughts on this country's actions

Blame my distrust on this country's
Broken creations of faux unification.

How dare you ask me to forget?
How dare you assume,
I will forgive for your conscious to reign clear.
Rape my ancestors without remorse.
Burned at stake, taking life, not yours.

Hangings for a picnic lunch spectacle?
You tell me to get over it. GET OVER IT!
WHAT THE HELL IS WRONG WITH THAT LOGIC?

Tell the JEWS to get over Hitler.
Tell the Jews to get over the gas chambers.
In that same breath, tell them to forget the Holocaust.

How can I forget,
My people packed like sardines in a can,
Brought to a land, to work,
Treated as chattel, slaughtered like chickens.
How can I forget?

Knowing that my people were sold
Like shoes to be worn and used as you saw fit.
How can I forget when daily,
We are regarded as being lazy and loving welfare recipients.
What happened to ROSEWOOD, WILMINGTON, and TULSA?
How can I forget? How do we forgive? That is the question of the day?

I Need a Strong Black Man

Yes, I am educated and can do for myself.
But I need a strong black man.
Yes, I own my own house and drive a nice car.
But I need a strong black man.
Yes, I can be independent.
But I need a strong black man.

NO, I can't do what a man can do and do it better.
I am a woman, and I need a strong black man.
Bring me your tired huddle mass struggling to break free,
From a society that can't see the potential that I see
Cause I need a strong black man!

My protector, guide, my spiritual eye...
I need a strong black man.
I see you in all your glory,
I know, and I feel your story...

I feel your pain and all that you wish to gain.
I need you, a strong black man.

Our sons are calling your name;
Our daughters need to see you plain...

I need you, strong black man.

Lay your head on my breast and find your rest.
No matter what the world is all about...
NO laws or subliminal thoughts will eradicate my head of state.
I am the queen, you are my king, and we are the royal court.

Yes, I am independent
With a home driving a nice car
But never from my lips nor in a breath
Will I say anything less...

I need you, strong black man!

Rest upon me your burdens
Rest on me in the midnight hours
To face the world in the morning
That wishes to devour
My strong black man.

With all the wrongs this world has done.
Lynched, beaten, pimped, and dignity stripped

I need you, strong black man, for I know your story.
I, too, have felt your pain.
Together we stand, sayin' never again!

Evalina

I am more than a descendant
From the slave trade...

I am the answer to prayers prayed.
The promise of a better tomorrow

I am my ancestor's promise land.

I am the freedom fought so many years ago.
I am the child of freedom.
A child who grew without the shame of shackles

I am the granddaughter generations descended
From a quiet secret scholar
Who hid their knowledge of reading
Yet passed it down generations to generations
The essence of education.

I am the granddaughter generations descended.
The entrepreneur and land cultivator

I walk their land playing in the fields that they planted.

I am the daughter who walks
Head held high and proud...

For within me are my ancestor's
Struggles for a better day.

I am the promise; I am the dream.

I am the answer to ...

Prayers prayed in the middle passage...
On a cold Georgia night
After planting fields sun up to sundown

I am the daughter of countless men and women
Who paved the way for me...

I am the daughter of my parents.
Who didn't want to be defined by those times...

I lay honor at their feet,
I am more than they could ever dream...
I am their future that they wished to see.

Through my eyes residing in my, DNA is
The feet of those before me that
Endured the anguish of the past

I lived their dream...

ABOUT THE AUTHOR

She gives honor, to her creator for life, the honored ones before her for their sacrifice, her mother and father for wisdom, and to her husband a life partner who empowers her as a woman. May these divine connections continue to cultivate what is needed in this world of existence.

Eman Nepay, born in Nebraska, is a scientist, historian, an avid reader who loves to write and enjoys learning. She is a wife and a mother. She lived most of her life traveling throughout the United States and overseas.

I AM BLACK is a collection of poems Eman has written from her adolescent years to the present day. She resides with her husband and children in Georgia and is currently writing her next publication that will be released by iSeebookz Publishing LLC.

* 9 7 8 1 7 3 4 7 7 6 2 4 9 *